Angel Fire

Angel Fire

Poems by *JOYCE CAROL OATES*

LOUISIANA STATE UNIVERSITY PRESS
BATON ROUGE
1973

142803

The poems published here have appeared previously in the
following periodicals, sometimes in slightly different
forms: *Antioch Review, Boston Review of the Arts, Carolina
Quarterly, Contraverse, Esquire, Literary Review, Little
Magazine, Mademoiselle, Malahat Review, Massachusetts Review,
Mediterranean Review, Modern Poetry Studies, New Letters,
Nine Windsor Poets, Ohio Review, Poetry Northwest, Prairie
Schooner, Prism International, Quarry, Red Clay Reader,
Salmagundi, Saturday Review, Southern Humanities Review,
Southern Review, Southwest Review, University Review, Windsor
Review.* To all these, acknowledgment and thanks are due.

ISBN 0-8071-0222-9
Library of Congress Catalog Card Number 72-91789
Manufactured in the United States of America
Designed by Albert R. Crochet
Second printing

for Jerome Mazzaro—
critic, poet, friend

. . . Ours is the universe of the unfolded rose,
The explicit
The candid revelation.

—D. H. LAWRENCE

Contents

PART III *Revelations*

Part I

LOVERS' BODIES

Lovers' Bodies

in every American city
the profane heavy beat
of someone's affection—
radios in automobiles speeding
narrowly in the street

love public as the bodies
of lovers
stalking everywhere
parading
the sidewalks crowded
doorways jammed
body upon body shouting
all the words
of love

flags of all commercial sizes
mourning dead leaders, or fathers
in the front yards of American streets
or cemeteries blotched with geraniums
always the damp pulsing of flags
the fluttering of rotted cloth

and the beat
of something growing—
filling in holes
filling in eye sockets—

the visible universe
collapses
and repeats itself
in our bodies:
all visible things
repeat themselves
into permanence

The Small Still Voice Behind the Great Romances

to see the sun slide over the edge
of the continent!—I always wanted that urgency
at the edge of satiation
I was always impatient with mornings
and the long capsuled stretch of the day
those rehearsals of hours to be endured
after the deaths of heroes
time like blocks of stone monuments
baked pale and unloving and permanent—

to see the reel run wild, the film
torn off its track!—I needed to die
so I fell in love
at the center of my vision a figure appeared
on target

juggling whorls of light
the sparks of my dreaming ignited his
his words, once ordinary, took on the darting precision
    of small crabs
poison-green in agitated water

the spheres of our dreaming came together

wanting to die
to lie down with the rocks
I lay down instead with a man
wanting to feel the heavy rocks against my thighs, aching
I felt instead the boulders of his giant manly fears
our skulls were crushed together
a rock-slide covered us
but was only dust: we blew it off, rising
new as actors

wanting to die
to feel the sickening wobble of the earth
my bowels cringing to be pierced eternally
I was pierced only by something human
wanting to die in an explosion of dust and rock
I died only in moods
and ascended again
humanly

Contrary Motions

you are the rising
the pump handle flung up
like a male shriek

I am the sinking
the draining of dark water
back to the private well

your eye in its solid liquid
moves in the socket
sure as grease

icy winds
cascade along the fish-strewn shore
of Lake Erie: ice like teeth

pellets of ice loosed and biting
teeth melting back to droplets
of harmless saliva

the edge of the ice retreats
to shore   on the break-water
the water-line drops

the empty forms of winter
smudged as thumbprints
fill in again heavily with life

At This Moment

at our touching
out of the alarm of our bodies' close touching
there strides on the window ledge
a gray-white bird
fragile-legged and ready to stab
like all birds
lovely in the blank
dumb alarm
of the eye

the bird is a surprise
and a perfection
like this moment in which we touch
exploring the moment
never lived before

at our touching
which is a groping in immense light
the bird will take shape strong
as the daytime air of this room
its small coiled neck
its eyes that seem sightless
its soul somehow pinched inside its beak
this bird declares its shape to us
perched at that magical point
at which our lives touch
like our bodies

Where the Wind Went Crazy

the tops of the palm trees are smashed
palm leaves hang down, shredded
limp and light as threads
the trunks like concrete
that never lived

mammoth towers
uninhabited

I feel the two of us grown to
mammoth towers
our heads dizzied by the height
time is piled beneath us
blocks pushing us up
there is a motion of nerves between us
strung between us like wires

lovers, we need no hurricane
to make war upon each other
and each cell of our living tissue
is at peace

Dancer

my mind is making me perform
strange dance steps
baroque designs with the toes

    lifting: the tense weight of my body
    the arching of the foot, which has its own brain
    the muscles of the ankle, no longer bone
    the stretching of the spine to a stalk

is it a stranger's energy
that so transforms me?
he possesses my body
with his rage
the blood-rimmed eyes are his
the opening and closing of his fist
of a heart

I feel this stranger up inside me
forcing me into a new shape
distending the skull
the obstacle-leaping legs
stretching to pain
the feverish thin flesh
ribs circling ribs
breath hard upon breath—

his rapture in this dance blooms
out of my toiling
constant over-leaping of my shadow's height
the dance pitched to fever
the dark membrane stretched tight
to constrain the soul
burst at last

At Our Fingers' Tips There Are Small Faces

concise whorls of flesh
fine as hairs
circling one another in a puzzle of lines
that would describe us unmistakably
and eternally

we stare into the small faces
a universe of tiny flesh
if gouged inside-out they would reveal
a deep red richness of flesh
minute bleeding in the labyrinth of flesh
and all the secrets of all the crevices
in our heads or in the rock of the earth—

but our fingertips are closed
secret and silent as ourselves
hidden as our eardrums
they touch lightly the winter air
and like the air they are barriers
protecting one world from another

A Woman's Song

Pounding of waves into my ears
pounding of pile drivers on the river
and pounding of cars through puddles
    on the undrained highway
pounding
pounding of waves flaring from hoses

    the bright shot of fire
    the shot of white water
    a ring of faces flashing
    men in firemen's costumes
    waves flaring from their hoses

at dawn
shutters fly open with a crash
I cry out, "Come here!"
I lie in the wild field beneath windows
I cry out, "Come down here!"

they shade their eyes with care
hands split their faces in two

Pounding of pulses at the horizon
the dip and rise of the treeline
pounding of wheels
cars passing over loose roads
horses' heads thumping angrily against stable doors
"I have children for all of you!"

children fall in clots in water
blood flushed safe to the river
pounding in daylight beneath
the solid passing of cars

Structures

inside a square foot of gravity
I am weightless as a child's steel toy
the flesh throws itself against the frame in anger
and the steel gives lightly, an inch
and then springs back—
the structures surrounding us
breathe with us, invisible
in this public place you sit
on a kind of throne
a stone bench
there is a plaque by a fountain, unread
and so the place is mysterious
you smile at me
there are yards of chaste grass between us
I study you in turn with the shyness
of centuries
the sockets of your eyes are hard
the bones of your face hard with thought
you are loving me in your head?
I feel my bones light as cheap metal
turned in your fingers, balanced, weighed,
inspected . . . .
I have no weight
gravity eludes me
as you lift me in your curious fingers
what are you always thinking?
you are bitter at not being infinite
and you will punish me
if we love
with a hand, a limb, an organ of despair—
because I am finite and contained
in a square foot of earth
you will hate me after
your loving concludes
you will pass finitely through me
through the structures we inhabit

Hate

the instinct of saintliness, its purity
unneeding intimacy
no touch
no crowd of shadows
clattering particles descend
in a dull drift upon us
last year's seeds
all morning, all month, in abstract hours
seeded to a dry embryo
that will never kick its way
into any dance

love is prodigious
as those flying fluff-balls of seeds
a waste
swarming and veined with gloss
expectant as the tart surface of the eye
no economy
no purity

in hate, we are arranged neatly
in tiers of seats
we watch closely
we are not intimate with the dying
since we cannot own anything
even our own bodies elude us, like theirs
elude us in dying

my love, you are another noun now
you have redefined the limits of my body
now no zone contaminated
the map is readable and ordinary
the needle rests at zero
in a sanctity
of hate

Insomnia

hounds charging from one wall to another
the beating of crazy wings
something at the window
tapping like glass upon glass

sleepless, my eyes have clouded over
I remain myself
there is no descent tonight to the cemetery of sleepers
no mingling of arms and legs
lazily lost in that element

I stare upon the self that is me
imprisoned in a box of four stark walls
panic rises sparkling along the legs
feathery behind the knees in that most intimate of places

I lie in bed symmetrical as a figure
on a ship's prow or on a tomb
hands folded in the caution of insomnia
the ache of being is everywhere in this room
ache of self like twine tightened around the head

we were born to drown in a blizzard of dreams
and sleepless, we are giant eyes
sleepless, we are protuberances
on the surface of the night
irritating the natural contours of the earth

Bloodstains

we are bloodstained women growing fiercely
up out of girls:
the armholes of our dresses tight
collars tight to bursting
against the muscular blue veins
our buttons hanging by threads
the fronts of these cotton dresses straining
across our breasts

so damp with blood
we fear
the muzzles of dogs will dip
into us

we are bloodstained women
stained with flecks of rust from the sky
soot from the sky
soot from the automobiles that rush
like men
everywhere in our sight
on the main streets and along the railroad tracks
and in the windy fields where grass grows
shooting up through the wheels

here we are stained with splashes
of old food and old love
the various smears of cherished pieces of junk
we have never known each other
we are bloodstained from common wounds
but we have never known each other
we belong to men and answer to their last names
though we have wiped our hands often
upon each other
we have never known each other
and we are so damp with blood
we fear the muzzles of dogs
will dip into us

Unpronouncing of Names

all the day of that rocky year
our bodies' shells beat helpless together
in seed-dotted brackish water
the elastic of our eyes rubbed

our fingers groped against the cages
of our ribs
our thoughts slid in and out of our heads
like fiery tongues of dragons

the silence in our bodies had no seams

it was a jellying love that slid
in and out of our bodies

then the water smoothed
we turned smooth as Sunday's light
the germs that had grown in the sore spaces
where our bodies rubbed lightened
and died in such innocent light

at the conclusion of the year
we learned each other's name
in the careful pronouncing of names
we undid the year's work

Several Embraces

I. OUR DEAD

nothing surrenders in the darkness of the head
that underworld of rantings and costumes!
nothing gives way
except to thaw small stinging terrors
minor enough in 1952
but now immortal

nothing surrenders:
Christmases resurrected
the tinseled branches crackling like flame
the skull a turmoil of monologues
nothing gives way
we age but not into adults
the brain is saturated with its jealous rantings
big paper flowers dusty with years
fragrant suddenly with the power
to make the heart leap

it is immortal, this rustling of childhood
the odor of damp wool
of sickrooms sour and pleasant
the disorder of blankets imagined as tents
the dampness of newspapers and a father's wintry embrace

nothing surrenders
there is no forgetting
the head is a net dragging decades
dust-balled and frayed and rubbery
nothing surrenders in the underworld of the head
always we wake in dreams to that old kitchen
we stare at old linoleum worn to immortal patterns
we are being gathered in the embraces of our dead

II. Two Bodies

filmy as the translucent skin of fish
we touched
we were encased in that moment
like words in stark inked brackets
set off from everything personal
that was not ourselves—
the sound of distant laughter
fleeting syllables beneath the threshold of sense—

in that autumn day the sun was white and invisible
bracketing us in the public glaze of the air
I think our love floated like reflections of birds
in the lake
the roots of trees in the water were not more giant
than our love
fish nosing through vegetation were not more doomed
in their element of fishly flesh
than we in ours, parting in two bodies

III. Fever

the breathing at your pores
clouds over with dots like tears
a Byzantine formality overtakes your long body
heat expands your elastic male arteries
as you stride upon the waves of the universe's
rocking blood

between your eyes another heartbeat pounds
your body shudders at the pitch
of the waves beneath your feet
red cells! white cells! magic digits we take on faith
imagining the high hot blood of our desire
red ants running wildly on our bodies

and then the two of us in this desperate embrace
are embraced by another
his figure darkly transparent
his breath unfevered and unshrill
his dark cool hands caressing our flesh in a mock prayer
a net of his arms outside the net of ours

he will deliver us
from the mad tuneful heat of blood
and bring the degrees of our blood
down
down to cerebral stone

IV. NORTH

his arms sink down around me
invisibly North rises like freezing steam

the brush of his face
a chest hidden against my back

there is an unseasonable chill to the air
the snow-touch of his fingers excites me
I must fight my way out of this embrace

the North slips down around us
rises vaporous through our ribs
ribs a maze of half-embracing circles
the air is aging
faces turn elderly behind their bright skins
it is so cold here that the roads gleam
steel-like with ice
there is nothing human to them
the air is so bright it yanks our voices
our lungs are coated with frost

we must fight our way out
of human embraces
making the calcium of our souls
hard as the cleanest Northern ice

Making an End

insisting upon the fifth act
the crescendo of footsteps and music
confused as star-specks of blood on a tile floor . . . .

insisting upon the deadliest of incantations
the unsaying of love, love's urgency
pronounced backward into silence . . . .

it is a fact of men in their maleness
the hunger for blows that silence words
speed and temperature at a crescendo
the fifth act and its extravagant whipping air
its tawdry symbolic costumes
its frayed velvet curtain

Where the Shadow Is Darkest

swinging in
to love again—
dropping away again—

time does not move for us
except in strange
lazy loops
tying us together—
releasing us
to the air's surface—

Our lives are two shadows
by accident touching
and where the shadow is darkest
there
we are together forever—

what we would forget
in our multiple selves
that darkest shadow recalls for us
and swings us strongly
to love again
together—

Part II

DOMESTIC MIRACLES

Domestic Miracles

* a stampede of hooves
must have bruised my thighs
in such iridescent designs

* a sweet rot rises
from the pages long dried yellow:
a diary warped now
unfamiliar even to my hand

* strangers' children swim
in the oil-streaked waves
their shouts and arms white
their joy like drowning

* my love: you make me permanent
as old unlovely busts of clay
unearthed in the Mideast
of forgotten people

in your presence my body thinks
something miraculous must happen

Our Common Past

you are something spilled darkly dripping
through the uneven floorboards of a house
floating up bits of dust and forgotten
sights from our past—

you have the feel
of being mortal
but the fluid of your life flows
and dries up and flows daily
you have been uncontainable
this hundred years
when you raise your hand in that random gesture
there are centuries of men in you—

you walk with me here
and the shadows of clouds skim
the pavement about us like lakes
like ghostly patches of water about us
your feet stride into everything
you are a flowing of phantom lakes
great dammed-up lakes ready to burst—

you blossom freely
in the maze of my body
there is no special mystery
for you to decipher
no dangerous surprise now
in our loving
this floating up of bits
from our common past

A Young Wife

In the scummy bowl the fish circle
curved like little fingers, barely

swimming, barely living, curved
slight as the turning-up of leaves.

Out there the weather streams, in here
the window-sill rises swollen

and nothing will lock in here, but
lies open as an uncupped ear.

The two-and-a-half rooms of our marriage
are filled with crockery and furniture and clothes.

Curious, we circle this small space and press
foreheads together, thinking. I fight the old fear

of beasts crouched beneath a bed, patient
and shapeless as a child's fear,
bumping my thigh against this new bedstead.

A City Graveyard

Beyond the iron-barred fence
traffic moves quick
as the eyes of squirrels
treed in this block-sized park
of the dead
tidy and dried are the geraniums in their beds
heavy the odd stocky benches of wood and concrete

here, children cut through the graveyard
bound for home
cut-outs of pumpkins in orange and crude crayon, fluttering
quicker
than the leftover flowers
the tassels of artificial bouquets
the children's voices are unguarded

banked gently as the beds of bedrooms
are the graves' inclines
and the gravestones have the cautious empty stare
of civilized people
as people who are visitors here
walk slowly through the aisles
studious, reverent before the Latin words
the names and prophecies
personality gone impersonal

from the boulevard the unserious sighs of exhaust
from the children needle-thin shrieks
the dead have many powers
deadly their piled-up bodies, their powdered weights
deadly their incantations carved in stone
their fingers grasping blade-like, grassy at our ankles

if we touch each other by accident here
we recoil
our fingers fear intimacy, here
our eyes, here, slant away from one another
the dead have no power except their weight
their drain upon our gravity
our small tireless names
murmured in their voices

A Secular Morning

we felt the earth strain at its outward arc
our souls hesitated last night
in a fear of plunging

now morning pulses us awake
the tissue of our hearts
secularized
reviving with daylight:
restored to visions on the correct
side of the eyelid

in the rooms of this morning we will encounter
forms primitive as those of the dark
but now named
shaped to fit the contour of a hand
weighed   measured   invented
like all objects of day

but the dark's silence vibrates in us
in our names for each other
the syllables seized to be relearned
rewon
hard isolated syllables of sound, cell-like,
atom-sized
unkillable

Leaving the Mountains

there are darts of final light
flashes like nerves' spiny ends
as the mountain road loops
in perfect rhythm
from right to left
left to right
and back again
again like the pattern
of the windshield wipers
left to right
as you guide with both hands
our slow car careening
out of this day-long dream
of mountains and spiky trees
and rock

the dream is of narrow roads turning
turning as in a dream
soundless upon themselves
and back

in the dusk of mountains
the car's headlights are faint
like our breaths, like our eyesight
ruined with wonders
that have aged us back into them
—the contours of mountains
small enough to navigate
but glaring red and orange and bizarre
as Mars
where the language would not be ours

guiding us out of a dream
you bring us sleepy with dread of falling
down out of the mountains
to Knoxville and a human night

Mile-High Monday

in that perpetual curving from us
we accelerate

the planet's motions draw us forward
material sucked out
by the speed of our passage
accelerating
on an empty road

is all space so empty?
must we fill it with ourselves?
the billboards of this scrubland
announce its emptiness
signs announce distances
stark unimaginable numbers
no one can conquer

we will become abstract, then
like all human achievements

Monday dawns hot and dry
Monday fuels us with an energy
set for the ocean
where we will cry, bewildered
What, is it over? Our continent over?

but this morning propels us
a mile high
we see no edge to the world

Angel Fire

the sun in a spasm
rocks the car
in this celestial scream
we flow together
mutely

better than marriage!
both of us slick with sweat
eyes aching from the glare
everywhere the world shimmers
with a false sunset
at every horizon

we have not spoken for a hundred miles
as if finally we have become a single flesh
and the flesh sighing with heat
Have we been experimenting with two bodies,
thinking ourselves two bodies?
every pore of our flesh has opened
unresisting
every pore breathes in this fire
spasm of light radiant
as pain
so bright you can't feel it

look, the fire gives another life
to the insects smeared on our windshield!
as if in celebration of our marriage
of heat

mauled by such fire
we are the only inhabitants
of this desert universe
the angels direct their fire to pierce
our eyelids
to penetrate the old selfish tightness
of our single selves
now no vision remains
to turn inward to a single name—

time is only the passage of light
the straying shadows like charred bodies
shapes like large grazing animals
on the mountains
or patches of shivering grass
that appear dangerous

    we have been experimenting with our separateness:
    unsolid bodies that imagined immortality

this fire holds nothing human
the angels in their passion
their belled-out cheeks
their hair dense as flames
hands that strike our faces palm to cheek
to awake us to this marriage of flesh
angels shouting
with the wind outside the car
shouting walls of heat
the slow explosion of heat at every horizon
staggering the rock of mountains
the rock glowing at its peaks
like lava
ancient breathable lava
angels struggling in the shapes of fire
younger than we
more vicious
their fire original and clean as music without words
killing the old selves of us
the old shadows
in one radiance

Part III

REVELATIONS

Firing a Field
—in memory of Flannery O'Connor

Unbelievers, look! there the taut darts of flame
unravel the landscape
the farmer and his boys herald the blaze as if
it were something of daylight
not night

Who can follow us into such meanness?

not night
not the fact of the fleeing mice
the grouse storming up into noise
the applause of the flames
crackling at the underside of the head

after this burning
the rabbits won't appear stark and brazen in the gardens
the porcupines will whine in exile
        licking their scorched feet
the insects' buzz will be silenced for hours
the slovenly moths and their wings of white-beaten gold
mute with defeat
mute with defeat
all the unbelievers
by their own good manners repelled
from our meanness

Who can follow us into such meanness?

after this burning
and the field stubbled with black weeds
punished for so much sunlight
and the cartwheels of butterflies loving
        in broad daylight
bug-loving orioles scattered back to the trees
the love songs of ants roasted crisp
and small soft gray animals beaten limp as rags
water-soaked in panic

let all things lie loosely dead!
after this fire that darts from our fingers
the groundhogs' burrows no blacker than the natural earth
toadstools soft as Christ under bare feet
our revenge sifts downward like falling ash
mightily
upon all creation

A Midwestern Song

The speaker is a young married woman,
having recently moved from the home of
her parents to the home of her husband.

here is the center of the world
and there is nowhere else to look
here is the center of the day
when the clocks yawn
it is the center of the continent, here
in this dry midwestern land
where breezes from the sea
lose their motion
where the tide flows out invisible
about our shoes

it is the center of a moment
I have lived before
when the air vibrates gently, ghostly
with cries of the sea

it is the center
of our bodies

my song is small and furious
as if maddened with salt-spray
the sting of seaweed stiffened out of motion—
Why do they offer me nothing more? Is there
nothing more?
Bored already with love as with
love's anatomy, I cry
Is there nothing more? What is possible, what
have other people possessed, what jewels,
what phoenixes, what lynxes tamed
for ladies' hands, devices jeweled
with crusts of blood?

the lawn around my home is an untrodden continent
the wind here has lost its rankness
its temperature is my own, so human
I hear a cry of seagulls, hawks, feasting birds
I hear the echo of these cries
I hear the pulsing of my own blood in my ears
ebbing to an inland temperature

Children Not Kept at Home

a mile down the road from us
      hidden from the road
there are children not kept at home

some of them bald
      their fin-like structures
hesitant as petals, the delicate

light of their eyes
      unsavage and mild
their faces masks of flesh

the Institution is not bricked up
      the children seem never to approach
the barred windows

in high-chairs they are kingly, queenly—
      saliva flies
their lives fly with the day, even

here behind the scabby vines
      even here their lives rise
with the day to ponder eternal souls

unable to walk
      some of them unable to speak or hear
legless or neckless beings yet eternal

a mile down the road in their special home
      unlived lives live
mildly for centuries

What We Fear From Dreams & Waking

I had a face on the front
of my head
a blank in which anyone might write
his name and address, city and state,
and the amount
of his enclosure.

I grew to normal height
a six-foot boy at eighteen
behind my face I had a shrewd fear
of living people
and the sudden illumination
of drugstore windows throwing light
onto sidewalks
or in doors opening
to friends' homes
I always feared
the nosings of animals
kept for pets
impostors like myself.

I awoke wrapped
in shelves of flesh
layered hot & stiff
as golden plates of armor
hugging the arms close
to the perspiring sides
the heartbeat magnified
eardrums sparkling in panic.

Unheated by my sweat
I imagine now the body of the dream
shaped squatting on my torso
the face unfleshed
unimagined
insulting amateur work
of a few minutes' hectic sleep.

Face bodiless in sleep
a body faceless fleshless at waking
I am begging you
not to turn from me
I am begging you for the imprint
of your face upon mine
hot enough to give me a face
to press upon me the features of a face
already proven to be human.

Acceleration Near the Point of Impact

the needles are starved, brown
fire-hazards warned of in the papers
but the evergreen rises miraculous
red- and green-glassed ornaments
at its peak a hand-sized-fluffed
angel

again the release of dirty snow
the melting rush of sewers
the church bells' ambitions
a Sunday of parades

rockets, ten-cent bombs
End of Summer Sales
bins of heaped-up bathing suits
their straps confused together
sandals and synthetic-leather backless shoes
with three-inch cork heels

and tactile November skies
by minutes and inches pushing us
into history

Family

What are we doing here jumbled
smelling of dust in a potato
sack? What is this dance we perform
sitting down? Tell me what are our faces
meant to declare, mashed together nose
against nose in friendly terror?

What is that word stamped faintly
on your forehead?—reversed blue ink
of an A & P melon? Oh in this crowd
it's a chore to breathe   to thrust a fist
through the bag to the dark
quiet cupboard—

Do we need so many elbows? so many
eyes crossing? Names leaping from mouths?

Why is it necessary to embrace
to make room? necessary to flatten the face
of stubborn signs? Why is the dance a jumble
of buttocks and calves
fingertips and eyelashes and stinging molecules
of sweat?

What are we doing here jumbled
for decades sharing the ache
of our dark back teeth? What is
the purpose of the dance? How does this
cupboard door unlock? Who has tied us
in here together and walked away?

How I Became Fiction

In the hospital I take care to walk
as if no destination threatened.
I drift with the cool metallic odors,
the creak of carts, the gala energy
of nurses arriving for duty
at eight A.M.

A yeast has arisen in my body.
Somewhere, a stranger's fate is being prepared,
to be typed out onto a form.

My body, see it is eager to please! and innocent
of its own yeast, its poisons and ungirlish discords!
Its product is being carried here
in a brown drugstore jar, prepared
for strangers who will not show offense.
They will charge fourteen dollars.
They will type up forms.

Death will not be simple, say the wheel-chaired
men, khaki-colored with the inertia of the wise.
They are mild beasts now, eyeing me.
Don't stare at me, I am not fiction!
Not your fiction!
My body is a girl's grown-up body, tugging
at their pinpoint eyes. My clothes are miserable
with the strain of possessing
this body so early in the day.

The men's eyes are fixed to me. But no darkness
would recover them, no alley make them male again—
Don't look at me, I am not fiction—
They were men once
but there is no proof of it now.
Unreal now, they brood over old skirmishes.

Like them I am drifting into fiction.
Like them I will be injected with heat and ice.
This morning, sweating, I await my fate
typed out onto a green form.
What further fiction is being imagined? What fee?

Things Happen to Us
—for Peter Wolfe

filling up with night
   things happen to us
     for long stunned minutes
       the thickness from ankle to knee
         filling in slowly, clogging
           like Socrates' death as it rose
             things happen to us in inches

bacteria humming up the body's side
   turmoil of their continents on our skin
     inside the perfect private skin
       filling with the songs of strangers
         filling with the hot bright sands edging oceans
         the night must rise to our height
       to press a face to ours
       lips to lips

memories swirl in their unstoppable currents
   this body is an unstoppable event
     filled to the distant ceiling of the skull
       with someone's shadow
       anchored
         like a winged statue
           above a celebrated grave

The Nightmare

She wakes from the pillow
body hammering to the hovering
above her
the withheld beating of wings

don't move

it is a whisper
she can't quite hear
she goes rigid with its certainty
a child's fatal sense
of proportion
don't move

a careless move will unhinge
the universe

in a network of nerves like wires
she lies rigid waiting
for the presence to withdraw
for the withdrawal of the vibrating
of dim sacred words passing
the noise of terror passing
the amorous wings fading
to daylight

Entering the Desert

a change of souls
a winter of abrasive silence
here, your weight will lighten
as moisture evaporates in savage patches
you know the envelope of your skin
thinning
in these gusts of unheated sunlight
a skin uncoarsened and unwise
like that of the desert trees
cunning as salt

in this air-rocked land
you look everywhere for a sign
your face reflected somewhere
the imprint of your features
so richly valued
in that other world

here, you are nameless
faceless
you want to cry *I am one*
with this mute whining wind
the perpetual dreaming sea
of sand
I am one with clouds as they transform
themselves unsuffering to shapes
slight as feathers
and then brutal as rocks
I am one with tough-fibered trees
whose white spines shiver
resisting speech

you want the equilibrium
of desert and self
you want the unforced flow
you want the desert itself
you want all the horizon and all the sky

but the desert is closed to you
it is too raw to absorb you
you are too human yet, your energies too human
too violent
entering the desert, you are yourself
entered and shaken and relearned

Mouth

That mouth. Enormous. Toothed
tusked smooth as piano keys.
It is an opening like sand
falling beneath your feet—
a surprise of a hole, falling away.

The breathing is drumlike.
In. Out. Moist as a cow's breath.
The warm wet panting
of a dog's muzzle.

Jaws that grip teeth. Teeth that
crowd teeth.
An idle coarse chewing of pulp.
The process begins at the rim
of the mouth.

Eager to be sucked into that crowding
from your far, dry self—
you acquiesce at the rim of the mouth.
You become this pulp
of yourself, this unnamed
noisy plasma.

The Secret Sweetness of Nightmares
—for Kay

Blocked
in your running—
pursued
by garments sweat-heavy
shaping themselves
to all the secrets of your body—

Failing to wake
as the heartbeat maddens—
failing to shout
the words of release—

You dip and rise
steeply in the waves
of your dreaming
your dreaming mouth
sour with terror
you have somehow earned—

You are still
inside your frantic turning
your ballooning words
expand your skull
heated to frenzy—

Yet the nightmare redeems
for it is everything you have accomplished
leading up close behind you
shallow footprints
it is in the finite shape
of your body as it lies, private
sweetened by a terror
no chaos
can interrupt

Becoming Garbage

hypnotized half
by its bulk
half by its permanence

hypnotized by the grit-
sized fineness of its glass
ungrindable beyond
visible molecules

absolute
as tiny gods
germ-sized
hard & cunning
as nails
ordinary
as the fake colorful tin
of cans

the contours of junk's mountains
do not beg the eye for a blessing
nor are tears torn from the eye
by its rusting spring bloom
godly in permanence because unmeltable
unbreakable
tough beyond what can be imagined
though once invented

smiling half
in and half out
a dream of such garbage
as we are becoming
the miracle that is unmeltable
unrottable
smiling we become our fates
the smallest living slices of tin & glass
our lungs will eagerly adapt
to the sweet golden poisons
immortal
while grass
grows old and dies

Prophecies

When he climbs out of the space
beneath the house
when he climbs into the house
he will be very hungry
so abandon the geometrical precision
of packages and bled-out limbs of animals
abandon the chain-locks
he will be very hungry

the profile-enhancing bulbs of your electricity
will show how he is comely
or ugly
but he won't notice
he will be very hungry
so abandon

the cameras
and shy away past your fireproof drapes
the Botticelli reprint
the noise of his personality is a noise of jaws
his eating is a motion of music
but he won't notice
because

his grown-up family have rushed in
hungry
in the space between two rushed beats
in your blood
they have erupted

take note
and shy away upward
in cautious grace up the stairs
how else to draw them to you
how else
the music of jaws drawn celestial

but be patient and shy
and fearful:
they are very hungry

at the far corner
    of the eye
there, there he is waiting

delicate as an eyelash
as the structure of an eyelash

waiting, the eye tenses
    in old selfly caution
waiting to see what it
    lacks seeing

Love, is it love
    waiting?
the lover already
loving
but waiting to be
    loved?

Southern Swamp

at the top of the skull the sky pours in
white bodiless heat
pours down the length of the body
the ancient planet emerges: water and trees and birds
long-necked as snakes

our blood inches upward as it heats
minutely upward, up
an unplanetary heat sears
an image into us:
long-necked birds
white, silent as snakes
silent as if their flesh
were only a husk of feathers

dream-soft
unformed

falling for decades through such a dream
you strike no bottom, no rock
or pavement
no limit to the falling
drifting downward as in sleep
unfathomed magic of dreams
the sighing of the palm trees
hand-like motions of their giant leaves
caressing you to sleep

        Then you wake
to your sudden need
to wake   to writhe in waking
the spasm of waking
unharmonious waking back
to unharmony

Elegy of the Letter "I"

—for Dan Hughes

child-shapes in the waves beckoned
hands churning into foam
grit uncrystallizing into shapes of faces
"Don't abandon us, come
to us,
ignore the landscape
hard-tasting dust and ugly rocks and peasant-faces—"
and I smiled enchantment
self-selfly-enchanted

centuries saw me running along the filmy coast
running through the film haloing harsh things
my heartbeat glided through them
nothing slowed me down, dragged my foot
if human fingers grasped my wrist I squirmed free
Oh I loathed them!—inside my filmy smile
which was never photographed

fig-trees were coarse tricky shapes
except in mist
which improved them
the morning dissolved into hot baths of sun
unless my eyelashes resisted
I cried to the sea, "Will you take this slave
of Music, this slave, slavish to thee, enslaved
to Thee, to the swimming dream of Thee
I have invented . . . ?"

water dense and mottled with foam
ugly as peasants' beards

the faces I loved were one face
hazy glimmering iridescent with my music
my dream of a smile glowing
dreaming
my smile reflected on the ugliest of faces
and therefore my miracle

Don't fear me!—don't fear my music
don't fear sea-salt-drops
just taste them as tears
unvialled but still sacred

How I loathed the boat that fought
to stay living
the top-sails thundering in protest!

but my schoolboy jacket was weighted
Lamia on one side
Aeschylus on the other
as the waist-down flesh struggled to float
I loathed the struggle
loathed
the noisy complex foundering
the unmusic of the sea
loathed the resisting world
unloving
uneager to take me in

only a perfect dream drew me down
which I will summon to you
I dreamt of my dearest Self:
lying on the sea-bed, calmed
on one elbow, lying calmed of struggle
sweet-rotting iridescent teeth
eyes sightless and pure
purer than those famous pearls
of eyes
Oh stubborn in purity in loathing
under the glassy cool translucent wave
we sing undirtied to you
listen
I dreamt the dreaming of my dearest dreamt Self
I dreamt   *He dreamt*
I sighed   *He sighed*
I wept   *He wept*

I go on till I am stopped
and I never am stopped
save by the ugly rocks
at Viareggio

City of Locks

there
in the bright ignorant air
the streets are crudely named:
    Canal Street
    Lock Street
    Water Street
    Plank Road

'the world's largest single span bridge'
is jumbled today with shoppers' cars
along this mile of the Erie Barge Canal
there are juttings of rock long blasted open
rock faces with mouths and eyes long blasted out

at Lockport, New York, at the famous locks
there are rusted railings painted over
the confused apparatus of workmen
always repairing the water's damage
there is the sullen soapy spouting of water
through a five-foot pipe

evilly, an odor rises from the bubbling fall
of one artificial level to another
old municipal buildings at the canal's edge
sink down to its silent strata
as if to a past before history

water flows through us today, warmly
through the citizens of Lockport, New York
and through us
in a small foaming series of falls

no fish glide farelessly beneath the stagnant
wash above the locks
the shadows of birds sink without sound
no dead citizens float gazing downward here
or cavort in the man-made falls
there is no orchard of seaweed and moss to refine
the canal's sludge to lace

eye to eye with the broken windows of warehouses
across the canal
we wait
wait for something to become clear—
but nothing happens
in these meager cities of our childhoods
nothing is declared

Revelations in Small Sunbaked Squares

hillsides of houses
hazy and still as the hillsides
of small graves
reel to us as the hills dip
inhabited in the hot slanted light
by inhabitants not visible
in this low-lying swamp of exhaust
  and another wave of hills
sunbaked squares of wall and window
the pressure on our eyes of a half-mountain
pert and squat the small perfect buildings
we are strangers to this city
hungry to interpret
the raw uniform bone of its hills
the treeless reeling streets
hills clung to
by coops of human invention
the neuter passage of windows
and now a trio of hills to the east
rises slowly to real or mistaken
graves sinking back to houses
thumb-nail-sized coops
streets like twine
  and the mind is fierce to translate
as the hillsides emerge endlessly
patient in miniature
eternal in the acrid glow
sunbaked sunglowing squares
of a great American city
if we longed for a dull infinity once
now we stare in awe at the finite map
of human streets
human bodies imaginable there
beyond our imaginations
urgent and finite in mysteries
beyond our judgment

The city in our heads
breaks from us
suddenly
swings from us   free
unconfined   unjudged
unwhole
unpossessed

Iris Into Eye

the spheres are whirling without sound inside
spheres
deft as ivory
tails of vertebrae interlock
hard as ivory and ice
it is a miniature sun frozen hollow

tails like the finest bodies
of fossils
are locked together
beneath the grainy surface of the skin
as the surfaces circle their surfaces

a ball of air circling itself
slicing the air slowly in its circling

daylight emerges as a small hole
an eye that achieves an iris
the collapsible space begins to breathe
the vertebrae lengthen into life

this sunless ether is silent
in every dimension
the sphere turns
I make my way up through layers of old bone
the ivory fossils of old blood
clenched fists of babies softened and unborn

coils are revolving
the hot fluorescent center of the globe vibrates
the speechless muscle of the brain spins slowly
slicing the air
continents shaping like raised welts
on the skin
the space between the ribs glows iridescent
warm as the most intimate mucous
of the soul

the eye widens
and now the iris becomes an eye
intestines shape themselves fine as silk
I make my way up through marrow
through my own heavy blood
my eyes eager as thumbs
entering my own history like a tear
balanced sacred on the outermost edge
of the eyelid